WHY
DOES MY NOSE
RUN

WHY
DOES MY NOSE
RUN

(AND OTHER QUESTIONS KIDS ASK
ABOUT THEIR BODIES)

JOANNE SETTEL
NANCY BAGGETT

ILLUSTRATED BY LINDA TUNNEY

ATHENEUM   NEW YORK

Library of Congress Cataloging in Publication Data

Settel, Joanne
Why does my nose run?

SUMMARY: Facts about human physiology in question-and-answer format, dealing with such phenomena as blinking, crying, burping, shivering, and sweating, as well as goose bumps, dizziness, pimples, allergies, and flat feet.
1. Human physiology—Juvenile literature. [1. Human physiology. 2. Body, Human. 3. Physiology. 4. Questions and answers] I. Baggett, Nancy. II. Tunney, Linda, ill. III. Title
QP37.B14 1985   612   84-21549
ISBN 0-689-31078-1

Atheneum
Macmillan Publishing Company
866 Third Avenue, New York, NY 10022
Collier Macmillan Canada, Inc.

Printed in the United States of America

Published simultaneously in Canada by
McClelland & Stewart, Ltd.
Composition by Dix Type, Inc., Syracuse, New York
Printed and bound by Fairfield Graphics, Fairfield, Pennsylvania
Designed by Scott Chelius

5 7 9 11 13 15 17 19 20 18 16 14 12 10 8 6 4

To Maya, Jenny, David
and all other kids
who like to ask questions.

CONTENTS

WHY
DOES MY NOSE
RUN

WHY DOES MY NOSE RUN?

Mucus, the gooey stuff that runs from your nose when you have a cold, is one of your best defenses against illness. There is always a thin layer of mucus in your nose, but when harmful germs get inside you and make you sick, your body manufactures large amounts of mucus to help fight the invasion.

Mucus is sticky like glue. It traps the dirt and germs that get into your nose or throat. Hundreds of tiny hairs called cilia help the mucus do its job. They lie just below the layer of mucus and are always moving. Acting like a long broom, the cilia sweep old mucus and dirt away from your lungs. This cleansing mucus travels up to your mouth where it is swallowed or to your nose where it is sneezed out. As the old mucus gets swept up, special structures called mucus glands are busy making more. When you get a cold, these glands work especially hard making extra mucus to help get rid of all the extra germs. It is this mucus that clogs up your head and runs out of your nose.

Sometimes, on a very cold day, your nose will drip even when you aren't sick. This doesn't mean that the mucus glands are producing extra amounts of their goo. The dripping occurs because cold air makes the tiny droplets of water in your nose come together or condense. The condensed droplets form big heavy drops, which run out of your nose.

RESPIRATORY TRACT

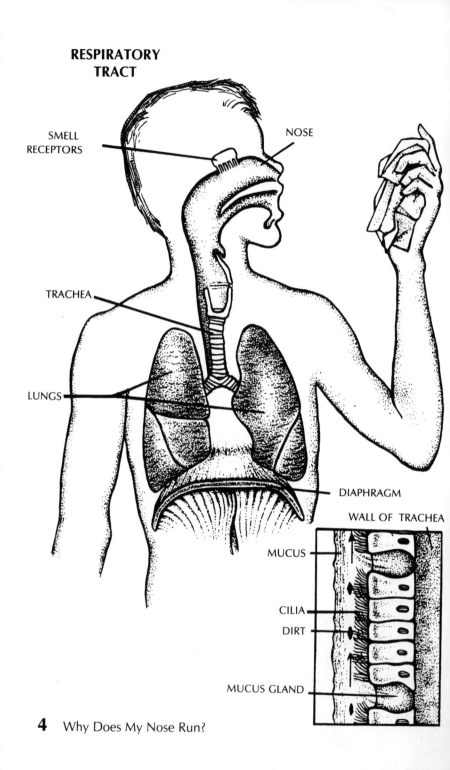

SMELL RECEPTORS

NOSE

TRACHEA

LUNGS

DIAPHRAGM

WALL OF TRACHEA

MUCUS

CILIA

DIRT

MUCUS GLAND

WHY IS IT HARD TO TASTE FOOD WHEN I HAVE A COLD?

It may sound silly, but the reason it's hard to *taste* things when you have a cold is that your nose is clogged up and you can't *smell* too well! Without even realizing it, you use your sense of smell right along with your sense of taste to examine and enjoy foods.

The fact is, our taste buds aren't particularly good tasters. There are about ten thousand of these tiny receptors on the surface of our tongue and mouth, but scientists say they can only sense four "flavors"—sour, salty, sweet and bitter. Because taste buds can only detect different combinations and concentrations of these four basics, they miss a lot of the appeal and flavor of food. (See page 57.)

As a result, our smell receptors—which are much more sensitive—help out with "tasting." We have about 100 million of these sensors in our nose, and they can recognize as many as three thousand or four thousand different odors! Very often, it's the aromas we pick up that give foods their distinctive, identifiable "taste".

Prove this to yourself with this little experiment. Have someone choose and mix up several different flavors of powdered fruit drink, being sure you don't see what colors they are. Now, with your eyes closed, hold your nose and carefully taste each of the drinks. Except that they are all sweet, you can't tell much about them, can you? Next, with eyes still closed, stop holding your nose and try again. The drinks have a lot more "taste," this time, don't they? And if you concentrate, you can probably tell what the flavors are.

WHY DO I SNEEZE?

A sneeze works like a vacuum cleaner in reverse. It gets rid of the dirt particles by blasting them out of your nose!

Sneezing is a reflex, under the control of an unconscious part of your brain. Any irritants, like dirt, chemicals or bacteria, that get into your nose can turn on the sneeze reflex.

The power of a sneeze comes from the air you breathe. When the reflex starts, your brain makes you take a very deep breath. This happens during the "AH-AH-AH," before the "CHOO," Then, the reflex makes your chest muscles squeeze your chest with tremendous force. Air is rapidly pushed up from the lungs and bursts out through your nose at speeds of up to 100 miles per hour! Irritating particles get carried out with the air.

The reflex that makes you cough is a lot like the sneeze reflex. It occurs when foreign particles sneak past your nose and into your throat and lungs. During a cough, however, air is directed out of the mouth instead of the nose.

WHY DO I STOP NOTICING AN ODOR AFTER I'VE SMELLED IT AWHILE?

When you come into the kitchen and something good is cooking, it smells great, doesn't it? But after a few minutes, no matter how hard you sniff, you can't seem to pick up that smell as well. It's as if your nose is bored and won't pay attention!

Actually, this is just about what happens. Once your olfactory, or smell, receptors get used to a particular odor, they just won't respond to it anymore. Scientists call this process "olfactory adaption." To understand how the process works, you need to know something about your sense of smell.

Unlike touching, seeing and hearing, smelling is a chemical sense. This means that in order for you to smell something, it has to give off minute particles, or molecules, of itself. A baking cake and simmering pot of soup release lots of molecules into the air, making them very "smellable." Iron and steel release few molecules, so they are virtually odorless.

When you sniff the air to smell something, molecules are drawn into your nose and up toward the smell receptors on its roof. These receptors are special, chemical-sensitive cells with tiny hairs that project out into the nasal cavity. When the inhaled molecules first come in contact with the hairs, the receptor cells quickly respond and fire off "smell" messages to the brain. Experts think that it may take only one molecule or, at the most, eight molecules to cause a cell to "fire." (See page 4.)

Nobody knows exactly how different molecules and odors are recognized, but some researchers believe that receptor cells can identify the shape, size, or electrical charge of molecules. In any case, once the smell receptors have sensed the same kind of molecule for a while, they just stop sending any messages. Although receptors may act as though they're "bored" with one scent, it doesn't mean that they're tired of smelling in general. Give them a new odor to sense, and they'll start right up firing messages to the brain. Then, you'll be able to smell the new scent clearly and distinctly—at least until your olfactory receptors get "bored" again!

WHAT HAPPENS WHEN I LOSE MY VOICE?

Your voice hasn't really been misplaced when you lose it! But it has been reduced to a raspy whisper or croak.

Losing your voice is called laryngitis. It occurs when your sound-making apparatus becomes inflamed and swollen. This can be caused by too much singing or loud shouting, or by an infection such as a cold.

The sounds of your voice are produced in the larynx, a boxlike chamber with an opening at the top and bottom. You can pinpoint the position of this muscular, fibrous chamber by pressing a hand against your neck while speaking. When you feel vibrations, you've located the "voice box."

Voice sounds are actually produced by strips of tough, stringy tissue called vocal cords. These lie across the top opening of the larynx. Like guitar strings, the vocal cords make sounds by vibrating back and forth. However, instead of being plucked, they are set in motion by air passing up through the voice box from the lungs. Also like guitar strings, the pitch of sounds produced by the vocal cords depends on how tightly or loosely they are stretched.

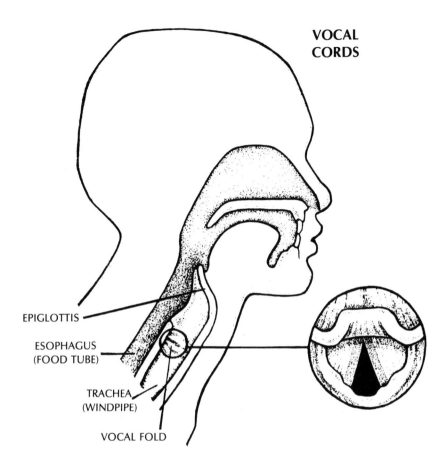

VOCAL CORDS

EPIGLOTTIS

ESOPHAGUS (FOOD TUBE)

TRACHEA (WINDPIPE)

VOCAL FOLD

For example, when you want to hit a high note, muscles around the vocal cords pull them very taut. When you're speaking in a low voice, the muscles let the cords go slack.

Since the vocal cords are made of very strong, flexible ligament-like material, you don't have to worry about snapping a string the way a guitar player does. But vocal cords *are* living tissue and so they can become irritated, inflamed and swollen.

When this happens, they don't vibrate properly, and produce only raspy, croaking or whispery sounds. Then you've got a case of laryngitis.

WHY CAN'T I HOLD MY BREATH AS LONG AS I WANT?

If you've ever vowed to hold your breath and not to let it go, you've probably discovered an interesting fact—after a minute or two your body ignores what you want to do and *forces* you to breathe!

The reason this happens is that you have a built-in system in your brain to make certain you breathe. With each intake of breath, your body obtains a rich supply of oxygen, the gas that your cells need to live. With each exhale, your body releases a gas waste product called carbon dioxide. Carbon dioxide is produced as your cells work and must be removed from your body. In fact, the job of carbon dioxide removal is so important to your body's well-being that the system controlling breathing can override even your strongest determination not to take a breath. Here's how it works.

As you hold your breath and halt the intake of fresh air, the supply of oxygen in your body starts getting used up and the carbon dioxide level rises. When this occurs, special carbon dioxide sensors called chemoreceptors notice and start sending warning signals to the brain. These signals stimulate an area called the inspiration, or air intake, center. Normally, when you aren't concentrating on holding your breath, stimulation causes the inspiration center to speed up breathing. But for a short time, you can keep the air intake center from responding just by telling yourself "DON'T BREATHE."

However, as time passes and the carbon dioxide level rises higher and higher, the chemoreceptors send out more and more warning signals. Finally, the inspiration center gets so many messages signaling it to "BREATHE, BREATHE, BREATHE!" that it overrides your command. Then, whether you like it or not, the stale, carbon dioxide-laden air is suddenly expelled from your lungs and you draw in a big gulp of fresh, oxygen-rich air.

WHY DO I YAWN?

That wide, wide opening of the mouth called a yawn may look a little silly, but it actually serves a useful purpose. Yawning is a simple, automatic step your respiratory system takes to help refresh your body.

To see how this works, think about yawning for a minute until you feel one coming on. Notice that as your jaw muscles force the mouth open, your chest cavity expands and you inhale a large gulp of air. The fresh air increases the level of vital oxygen and lowers the concentration of waste gas, carbon dioxide. This gives your body a little boost.

Yawning is a reflex action of your respiratory system. People often think a yawn means you're bored or tired, but usually it's just a sign that you've been sitting quietly and breathing shallowly. This is why you don't normally yawn during vigorous exercise even if it's very tiring. You may also start to yawn when somebody else does, although no one really knows why yawning seems to be contagious.

WHAT ARE HICCUPS?

Nobody likes to have them, there are dozens of ways to get rid of them, and they sometimes make other people laugh. They're hiccups, and you get them whenever a breathing muscle called the diaphragm goes on the blink. The large, flat diaphragm lies just under your rib cage and stretches from your belly to your back. By pumping up and down, this sheetlike muscle helps to move air into and out of your lungs when you breathe. The air travels in through your nose, past your throat and down a long tube called the trachea, which leads to the lungs. (See page 4.)

Hiccups start when the diaphragm moves up and down too fast. Air rushes into the lungs and the opening to your trachea, the glottis, briefly snaps shut causing a "hic" sound.

If you get the hiccups, the odds are good that you've been crying, laughing, or gulping down a meal. Anything, like swallowed air or large amounts of food, that causes a sudden stretching of the stomach, can lead to a bout of hiccups.

There are lots of tricks that you can use to stop an attack once it's begun. You can take a deep breath, breathe into a paper bag or take a teaspoon of sugar. If none of these methods work you can always just wait. Hiccups usually stop on their own after a few minutes.

WHAT ARE PIMPLES?

Pimples are caused by too much of a good thing! They result when your body's tiny oil machines, the sebaceous glands, dump an oversupply of fluid on the skin.

These glands normally produce a steady supply of oil, to keep your skin soft and smooth. Sometimes, however, they go haywire, causing pimples.

You can't see your sebaceous glands, because they're buried in the skin, next to the root of a hair. Every hair on your body sits in a pit called a hair follicle. Although you may not always notice the hairs, you can sometimes see the openings to the hair follicles, the pores, on parts of your face like your nose. (See page 25.)

Normally, the oil making sebaceous glands empty their slippery liquids into the hair follicle. The oils then flow up the hair and onto the skin. When too much oil is produced, however, this extra fluid doesn't get to its destination. Instead it plugs up the follicle. Bacteria grow well in the clogged follicle, causing the skin around it to become swollen and red and forming a pimple.

Although you can get pimples at any age, you're more likely to have them as a teen-ager. At this time in your life certain chemicals, called hormones, are being produced in your body in large quantities. These hormones not only cause you to mature, but they also make your sebaceous glands produce extra amounts of oils. Fortunately, your oil makers eventually adjust to the new levels of hormones and go back to normal levels of production.

WHY DOESN'T THE SKIN ON MY FOOT WEAR OFF LIKE THE SOLE OF MY SHOE DOES?

Actually, the skin on your foot *does* wear off! Every day a small amount of skin peels off the bottom of your foot. As your old skin peels away, however, new skin grows in to replace it. This daily process of peeling and growing occurs not only on the skin of your foot, but also on the skin of your hands, arms, legs and every other part of your body.

To understand how skin peels and grows, let's look at what it is made of. There are two main layers forming your skin. The outer layer, called the epidermis, acts as the body's protective covering. It is built from hundreds of tiny parts called cells. These cells are so small that you can't see them without the aid of a microscope. If you did look at your skin under a microscope, you would see that skin cells are stacked in rows like the bricks in a house.

Just below the cells of the epidermis is a layer called the dermis. It is here that you find the blood vessels that help keep your skin alive and healthy. These vessels carry blood to your skin and to every other part of your body. Blood supplies the skin cells with food and other important things that they need to live. (See page 25.)

The epidermis of your skin is always growing. Skin cells continuously split in half to form new cells. These newcomers are formed at the bottom of the stack, very close to the blood vessels. Old skin cells are at the top of the stack, far away from the blood supply. As more and more new cells form, old cells get pushed farther and farther away from the blood vessels. Soon, the old cells at the top of the stack are too far away to get the food they need. The old cells harden, die and eventually peel off. You can see this peeling when you get a sunburn. The burn makes skin cells die rapidly, and large clumps of cells come off at the same time.

WHAT CAUSES WARTS AND MOLES?

Warts and moles may seem similar because they are both funny-looking, bumpy places on the skin. However, they are caused by different things.

A wart is a lump that occurs when certain kinds of viruses enter your skin cells. These viruses cause the cells to grow and multiply rapidly, producing the raised area you notice on the skin surface. The commonest type of wart usually looks whitish and rough-textured on top.

The viruses that cause warts can spread from one place to another, producing more funny little lumps. There's no need to worry though, because warts are harmless. And if they become bothersome or unattractive, the doctor can remove them or can recommend an ointment to make them dry up and disappear.

A mole is also a skin growth, but it is not caused by a virus. Most often, moles look like small, raised brown spots. The presence of moles seems to be determined before birth, but no one is really sure what makes them occur. Often, moles appear during childhood, and a person may have between twenty and eighty of them by the time he or she is grown!

THE WART

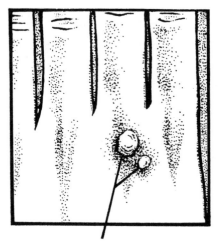

WARTS

Moles are usually harmless, although you should take care not to pick at or irritate them. If they do become irritated, or grow rapidly, or look different than usual, make sure to mention this to your doctor.

WHY DO DIFFERENT PEOPLE HAVE DIFFERENT-COLORED SKINS?

People just naturally come in a wide range of colors. Our skin can be nearly as light as vanilla taffy or as dark as rich chocolate cake. It can also come in many brownish, reddish or yellowish shades. Exactly what shade we are depends partly on our parents' skin color and the characteristics that they passed on to us. Our color also depends on how much the skin is darkened by exposure to the sun.

Whether our skin is light, medium or dark, much of its color normally comes from a brown material, or pigment, called melanin. Melanin is produced and secreted by special cells called melanocytes deep in the skin. You might think that dark-skinned individuals would have more melanocytes than light-skinned ones, but actually we all have about the same number. (See page 25.)

So why are some people darker than others? If we're born a darker shade, it simply means our melanocyte cells are very active and make a lot of melanin. Of course, skin can also turn dark from a tan. Exposure to sunlight stimulates the melanocytes to make extra melanin, which in turn provides a dark, protective screen against harsh sun rays. People who have very active melanocytes in the first place tend to tan more deeply and are less likely to burn.

Although melanin is responsible for the brown shades in skin, its yellow and pink tones have other causes. Yellow tones, which are often most noticeable in Oriental people, are produced by another pigment called carotene. Oddly enough, this material is the same one that colors carrots!

The pink look of the skin of extremely fair, light-skinned people is not the result of a skin pigment at all. It's simply the blood in the blood vessels near the skin surface showing through.

Now you know what causes the usual range of human skin colors. But if you've ever seen a person (or an animal) called an albino, you are aware that on rare occasions skin can be unusually pale or pinkish white. In this case, the eyes and hair are likely to be pale or pinkish as well. The distinctive appearance is due to the fact that albinos don't have any brown pigment, melanin, coloring their skin, hair or eyes. Their melanocyte cells aren't able to make any of this material because they are born without a special activating chemical, or enzyme, required for melanin production. Otherwise, though, they are just like everybody else!

WHY DOES MY SKIN TURN DARKER IN THE SUN?

A suntan is our skin's way of providing a sun umbrella for our bodies. When we're out in the sun too long, our own skin tries to protect us by forming a screen against harmful light rays. This screen is a tan.

The darkening known as tanning is caused by the coloring material in the skin called melanin, a substance that supplies the brown tones in our skin. The more melanin we have, the browner our skin will be. Exposure to the sun causes our bodies to make even more melanin than usual so our skin gradually turns darker.

The tanning process starts deep inside our skin in the special cells that make melanin. Called melanocytes, these cells are always making some of the brown pigment, but in response to sunlight they step up production. Sunlight also causes little particles of melanin to travel up and collect over the "heart", or nucleus, of cells near the surface of the skin. Scientists think that the reason melanin covers and protects the nucleus is because the nucleus contains some very important chemicals, or genetic particles, that control the normal growth and development of the cell. (See page 25.)

Despite what some people think, a deep tan doesn't really mean we're healthy. It's just a sign that our skin has been working very hard to protect us from harsh sun rays. Furthermore, experts say we shouldn't expect the tanning of our skin to do the whole job. Too much sun can cause drying, aging and even skin cancer, so it's wise to wear protective clothing, a hat and sun screen lotion whenever we're exposed to the sun for long periods.

WHY DO OLDER PEOPLE OFTEN HAVE WRINKLES AND GRAY HAIR?

Your skin is springy, like a rubber band. You can pull it, press it, or twist it, and it will snap right back into place.

The skin of older people is like a worn rubber band—it doesn't snap back fast or have much elasticity any more. This means that it doesn't stay smooth and tightly stretched over the bones and muscles. This causes some of the wrinkling. In addition, the fatty tissue under the skin that plumps it out becomes thinner as people age. Since some of this "padding" is gone, the skin sags, forming even more of the little folds we call wrinkles.

Loss of elasticity of the skin and wrinkling happen gradually over a lifetime. They occur at different rates in different people. However, being out in the sun and wind a lot causes extra wear on skin and speeds loss of elasticity. This is why people who spend their lives working outdoors often have lots of wrinkles.

Just as skin loses its springiness, hair loses much of its color as people age. Yes, that's right— strands that *look* gray or white are just ones that have lost their natural coloring materials, melanin or carotene. Nobody knows exactly why, but over time the individual cells that produce the pigment in each hair just get tired and stop making it. Since the melanin-producing cells stop working much sooner in some people than in others, certain individuals have a lot more gray hair than others. The timing for getting gray hair is set by our genes, and occasionally it happens when people are still in their teens or twenties!

WHY DOESN'T IT HURT WHEN MY HAIR GETS CUT?

When somebody yanks your hair, it hurts! This is because hairs are rooted in living tissue with nerves that sense pain. However, when your hair is cut off, you don't feel a thing. The reason for this is that the hair *shaft* (the part that you can see) has no nerves and is completely dead!

Yes, as awful as it sounds, those seemingly silky, shiny strands are really layers of lifeless, hardened cells! Here's how it happens.

Hair cells are formed in tiny, tubelike pits buried about one-eighth of an inch deep in your skin. These deep pits, or follicles, are surrounded by tissue containing both nerves and a nourishing blood supply. Within each pit, hair cells always grow and divide from the bottom upward. As these cells mature, they are gradually pushed up the length of the follicle by others developing underneath. At the same time, a tough protein material called keratin is added to these mature hair cells. (See page 25.)

By the time the old, keratin-hardened cells reach the skin surface and emerge as hair shafts, they are so far from the life-giving blood supply deep in the follicle that they have died. That's why you can bend, twist and even cut hair strands and —as long as the living "roots" aren't pulled—they won't hurt a bit!

WHY DOES SOME OF MY HAIR FALL OUT WHEN I COMB IT?

In case you ever worried about it, brushing or combing isn't what makes hairs fall out. They just naturally come loose and drop away. In fact, you probably shed seventy or eighty of them from your head every day! The reason you don't miss them is because there are about one hundred thousand others still firmly in place on your scalp.

It's easier to understand how hairs can loosen and fall out if you know how they grow in the first place. Each hair is individually produced in a tiny pit, or follicle, buried below the skin surface. In each pit the cells that form a hair grow from the bottom upward. Normally, these cells constantly grow and divide, pushing the older cells of the hair shaft up and out through the skin surface.

Every few years, however, the cells that form the bottom of the hair decide to stop growing and take a rest. Then, the part that's already formed gradually loosens from the base and is shed. After resting awhile, the cells in the bottom of the follicle crank up and begin dividing again. Soon there's a new hair growing out to replace the old one.

Sometimes, as people age, hair follicles that shut down just don't bother to start up production again. Then, thinning of the hair or baldness results.

WHY DO SOME PEOPLE SMELL BAD?

Did you ever smell so bad that even *you* didn't want to sit next to you? Maybe it was because you were very sweaty or hadn't had a bath for a while. Probably you found that a good shower and a lot of soap took all the smelliness away. Or did it?

Even when we don't smell bad to each other or to ourselves, we still smell! In fact, each of us has a special odor that belongs to us alone. Dogs, with their sensitive noses, can actually tell us apart just by sniffing.

It may sound a little gross, but the truth is that our natural odor results from millions of harmless bacteria, which make their homes on our bodies. These microscopic invaders nestle in the folds and creases of our skin, growing particularly well in warm, moist places such as the armpits.

Our minute companions first move onto our bodies during the process of birth. Then, each person who touches us—from our mother and father to our doctor and nurse—adds a little sprinkle of bacteria to the collection. This means that every one of us has his or her own unique assortment of bacteria. These tiny residents settle in and multiply, staying with us for the rest of our lives and giving us our own special scent.

Our bacteria stick around because our skin manufactures a continuous supply of food for them in the form of sweat and oils. Odor is produced when the feeding bacteria are breaking down their foods.

Although we can never get rid of all our bacteria, or our sweat and oils, we do remove some of each when we wash. Regular bathing keeps us from smelling bad to other people. Our dogs, however, always recognize our scent.

WHY DO I SWEAT?

Just like a house, your body has a built-in thermostat and a heating and air-conditioning system. Sweating is a part of the system that works to cool you. Becoming flushed, which often happens along with sweating, also helps keep you cool.

Sweating occurs automatically to help maintain the body's most comfortable temperature of 98.6°F. You always sweat some, even though you may not notice. The hotter your body gets, the more you sweat. If you're playing hard in hot weather, you often sweat pints or even quarts of fluid. Most likely, your skin will also flush—become very warm to the touch and perhaps look reddish.

SKIN

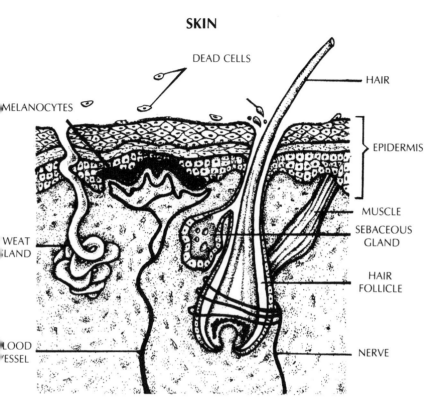

DEAD CELLS

HAIR

MELANOCYTES

EPIDERMIS

MUSCLE

SEBACEOUS
GLAND

SWEAT
GLAND

HAIR
FOLLICLE

BLOOD
VESSEL

NERVE

Let's see just how sweating and flushing keep you cool. All over your body there are tiny openings in the skin called sweat glands. There are two to three thousand of them in every inch of skin, and sometimes even more on your palms! These glands connect to tubes that loop and coil deep into the skin. Some of the fluid from around the blood vessels in the skin is drawn off into the tubes and then passes through the sweat glands to the outside. Then the sweat evaporates from the surface, cooling you by carrying some of your body heat away in the air.

You can easily test the cooling effect of evaporation for yourself. Put some water on your wrist. Then, fan the wet area or blow on it. There's a cool feeling, right? That's because the moving air speeds up evaporation of the water.

Sometimes when the weather is very hot, you can also tell that the evaporation process has slowed way down. This happens when the humidity is high and the air contains lots of moisture. Damp air slows the evaporation of sweat, making it especially hard for heat to be carried away. Then you feel extra warm and sticky.

Like sweating, flushing helps the body get rid of excess heat. Flushing is especially likely to occur when your muscles work hard or when you have a fever because a lot of body heat builds up then. The hotness and redness that characterize flushing are just signs that the blood vessels in the skin are opening, or dilating, and heat is being vented to the outside.

WHY DO I SHIVER WHEN I'M COLD?

Just as sweating is part of the body's air-conditioning system, shivering is part of the system that keeps you warm. An area of your brain known as the hypothalamus works like an automatic thermostat set at 98.6 degrees. The hypothalamus measures your blood temperature and if your blood gets too cold, this temperature control unit tells your muscles to shiver.

When you shiver, your muscles make heat. Actually, working muscles always make some heat. Every time a muscle cell breaks down a molecule of fat, carbohydrate, or protein to get energy, a little heat is also given off. Producing heat, however, is not usually a muscle's only job. Generally when your muscles are working they make you move. For example, you use the muscles in your arm to lift your hand, the muscles in your neck to turn your head, and the muscles in your face to smile. As your muscles move you, they also make a small amount of heat. That's why you feel extra warm when you do something active, like running or riding a bike.

When you shiver, your body moves only a little bit, yet lots of muscles are working. Your muscles do not have to work as hard as they would if they were also moving your body at the same time. Thus, shivering is a good way to warm up without using a lot of energy.

WHY DO I GET A FEVER WHEN I'M SICK?

Some of the organisms that make you feel awful when you're sick produce chemicals that mess up your body's temperature regulator as well. The chemicals, called pyrogens, work by resetting your brain's thermostat.

As mentioned in the discussions of shivering and sweating, your brain has a thermostat that is normally set at around 98.6°F. When your body temperature drops below 98.6°F, the thermostat makes your body warm itself. When your tempera-

ture goes above 98.6°F., the thermostat turns on your body's cooling mechanisms.

Pyrogens turn up your body's thermostat from its normal setting of 98.6°F. to a new higher setting. If your body's thermostat is set at something like 102°F., your brain will "think" that 98.6°F. is cold, and it will make you shiver to warm yourself up. Thus, you might feel chilled even though your temperature has already reached 100°F. Once your body temperature has reached its new setting of 102°F., however, the shivering will stop.

Some scientists believe that slight fevers may actually help people to fight off an illness. An increased body temperature is thought to make it difficult for harmful organisms to grow and multiply.

High fevers of over 106°F, however, can damage human body cells and must be brought down rapidly.

One way to reduce a fever is with aspirin or aspirin substitutes. These help to lower a person's body temperature by turning off the effects of pyrogens and resetting the brain's thermostat back to normal. Once reset, the brain's thermostat will turn on the body's cooling system, causing a person to get rid of his extra body heat and returning his temperature to around 98.6°F.

WHY DO MY EARS, TOES AND FINGERS GET COLD FIRST ON A WINTERY DAY?

Have you ever noticed the color of your fingers when they feel really cold? They should look pale. When it's cold, your body sends less blood to your fingers, and blood is one of the things that gives your skin its color. You can check this out on yourself by squeezing down along the length of your finger to push the blood out. Your finger will look pale for a few seconds until the blood returns.

By sending less blood to your fingers, toes, and ears, your body can keep the rest of itself warm. On a comfortable day blood carries heat from the center of your body out to the surface of your skin. Your warm skin then loses some of its heat to the air. Heat leaves your body fastest through your extremities, that is, the parts that stick out, like your ears, fingers and nose. When the weather is cold your body tries to keep heat trapped inside itself, in order to protect your sensitive organs.

It does this by closing off some of the blood vessels to your skin and extremities. Then the inside of your body can stay fairly warm even if the outside feels cold. If, however, your extremities remain without blood for too long, they can get frostbitten. When this happens some of the blood-starved tissues get so cold that they freeze and die.

In addition to redirecting your blood flow, your body also has a few other methods of warming itself. These include shivering and breaking down food stores to make heat.

WHY DO I GET GOOSE BUMPS?

The goose bumps that you get when you're cold or frightened are simply a sign that your hair is standing on end. Here's how it works. Every single hair on your body has its own tiny muscle. When your skin gets cold, the hair muscles contract and pull the hairs up. As a hair becomes erect it pulls on the skin around it, forming a tiny bump. (See page 25.)

To understand why our hair stands on end, it's necessary to take a look at what hair fluffing does for other mammals. Hair helps to keep furry mammals warm by trapping a layer of air against their skin. Hair that is fluffed up on end is very good at trapping air. So, when a mammal gets cold, its brain automatically sends a message to its hair muscles causing the hair to fluff. Our brains also make our hair fluff up when we get cold. Since we don't have much hair to fluff, however, it doesn't warm us very much when we do it. Why then, do our bodies bother? Probably because our long ago ancestors had thick hair all over their bodies. Hair fluffing would've helped them keep warm. Today, we still have the ability to fluff even though we've lost most of the hair.

WHY DO I HAVE WAX IN MY EARS?

Maybe you never thought that the waxy, yellow stuff in your ears is useful. But this sticky material, which scientists call cerumen, helps solve a basic problem of ear design—how to let sound travel in and keep everything else out!

Here's how earwax works. The outer part of the ear is shaped like a funnel to gather sound waves and direct them down a tunnellike canal to the eardrum. Since this outer area is open, it's possible for dirt, insects and other irritants to enter

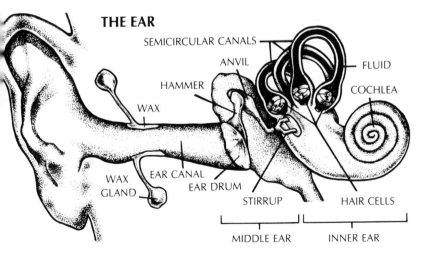

THE EAR

along with sound. To prevent this from happening, the canal is lined with tiny hairs and is coated with wax. The hairs form a screen and the earwax works like flypaper, trapping foreign objects.

Earwax is made by about four thousand glands along the inch-long ear canal. In some people, these glands produce only small amounts of wax. In others, they make a lot and it has to be removed from time to time. In fact, some people have so much earwax, the buildup starts to block hearing and has to be removed by a doctor!

Doctors say the best way to remove your own wax is to gently rub around the external part of the ear with a damp washcloth. It's unsafe to put anything into the ear canal to clean it. This might pack down the wax and make it harder to remove, or even worse, poke too far into the canal and damage the eardrum.

WHY DO I GET DIZZY WHEN I SPIN IN A CIRCLE?

Running, walking, jumping or watching TV are things you probably do without even thinking about them. But every time you move—or even just sit— a lot of work is going on inside you to keep your body from tipping over or falling down.

In order to keep you balanced, your brain needs to gather information about your body's position in space. It gets this information from several places. Your eyes notice the body's position and send the brain messages about it. At the same time, when-

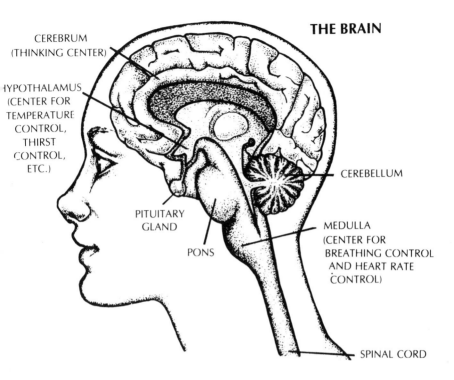

THE BRAIN

CEREBRUM
(THINKING CENTER)

HYPOTHALAMUS
(CENTER FOR
TEMPERATURE
CONTROL,
THIRST
CONTROL,
ETC.)

CEREBELLUM

PITUITARY
GLAND

MEDULLA
(CENTER FOR
BREATHING CONTROL
AND HEART RATE
CONTROL)

PONS

SPINAL CORD

ever you move, the muscles and tendons also send
messages, called proprioceptive sensations. These
tell the brain exactly what the muscles and tendons
are doing. A third thing that happens is that special
parts of you called the organs of balance sense your
body's motion and its position in relation to the
ground. The organs of balance send their signals to
the brain, too.

Normally, the brain sorts out all these messages and quickly decides what to do next. Then, it
instructs the proper muscles to "Tighten up!" or
"Relax," so you keep your balance. The process is
so efficient you aren't even aware of it. However,
spinning in a circle makes the brain's job even more

Why Do I Get Dizzy When I Spin in a Circle? **33**

complicated than usual. Because of this, you feel dizzy and maybe stagger around.

It's easier to understand what causes a feeling of dizziness if you have an idea how some of the organs of balance work. On each side of the head deep inside the skull are a group of three organs called semicircular canals. The canals contain fluid and have tiny hairs imbedded in their base. Every time your body changes position, the fluid shifts too, moving the little hairs. (See page 31.) By sensing the movement of the hairs, the brain keeps informed about your motions.

The problem with spinning in a circle is that it causes the fluid in the canals to shift around more violently and continuously than usual. As a result, the little hairs in the semicircular canals move a lot and many motion messages go to the brain. These make you feel as if your body and the whole world are whirling about. Also, when you spin around, the fluid is so stirred up that it "sloshes" back and forth like water in a bucket. And the sloshing continues even after you stop. This means the hairs keep moving, sending the brain motion messages when, in fact, your body isn't really moving any more.

Naturally, your busy brain can get confused by the conflicting information it's receiving. The movement of the little hairs in the semicircular canals says you're moving, but your eyes, muscles and tendons say you're standing still. When this happens, the befuddled brain may send the wrong directions back to your muscles, causing you to stagger around or fall down.

WHY DO I BLINK?

Blinking eyelids work for eyes somewhat the way windshield wipers do for windshields. They both move back and forth, keeping the surface clean. Windshield wipers are assisted in this job by fluid that is squirted out onto the glass. Similarly, your eyes are helped by fluid from your tear glands. A tear gland is a small almond-shaped sac located under the top lid of each eye. This gland makes tears, which are a mixture of water, salt and mucus. Small amounts of tears continually pass out of the gland and onto the top of your eyeball. When you blink, tear fluid spreads over the whole eye, washing off dirt, killing germs and keeping your eyeball from drying out. (See page 36.)

Actually, blinking eyelids work better than windshield wipers because they not only help to wash things out of your eye, but they also keep dirt from getting into your eye in the first place. Any time an object moves towards your eye, you blink automatically. Although your eyelids are too thin to keep large objects from hitting the eyeball, they do a good job of keeping out insects and bits of dust.

If you have ever noticed how dirty and dry a car windshield gets when the wipers stop working, you can imagine what would happen to your eyes if you stopped blinking. They would get dirty and feel terribly dry. Luckily, however, you can't stop blinking no matter how hard you try. If you don't believe this, stare at yourself in the mirror and try to keep from blinking. You can't, can you? This is because blinking is so important for your eyes that your brain makes you do it even if you don't want to! Thus, blinking not only helps to keep your eyes clean and healthy, it's also something your eyelids do on their own without your ever having to turn on a switch or worry about equipment failure!

WHY DO I CRY TEARS?

Your eyes make tears all the time, not just when you're unhappy. Each eye has its own special tear gland located inside the upper lid. The tear gland is like a faucet that drips all the time. This constant dripping releases a tiny amount of fluid that washes the surface of your eye.

Like any faucet, a tear gland needs a drain. The drain for tears is found in the inside corner of each eye. You can see the openings if you look in the

THE EYES

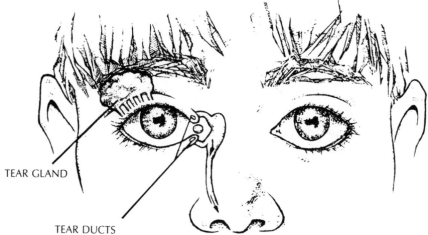

TEAR GLAND

TEAR DUCTS

mirror. Each hole leads to a small tube that lies under your skin and runs down to your nose. Normally, the fluid in your eye empties into its tear drain as quickly as it is made.

When you are sad, your brain tells the tear gland to make more tears than it usually does. The tear drain is not big enough, however, to catch all of the extra tears, so some spill out of the eye and onto your face. Additionally, because there is so much tear fluid running down the drain into your nose, you often get the sniffles when you cry.

Nobody is certain why people cry when they are sad. Scientists do know, however, why people cry at other times. Irritating chemicals from things such as sliced onions or a smoky grill make the tear glands go into action. The surplus tears help to wash the irritating chemicals away.

WHY ARE TWO EYES BETTER THAN ONE?

The best way to understand why we have two eyes is to take a look at the world with just one. If you close one eye and look at an object that's about a foot away from you, the object you see should appear to be touching the objects behind it. Now instead use both eyes; the world that you see will look very different. Objects will stand apart from one another, they will have depth. You can show how important this depth perception is in your everyday life by performing a simple test. Try to thread a needle with one eye closed. Now try again with both eyes opened. The task should be much easier using both eyes. The reason for this is that you can better judge the distance between the needle and thread when you can see their depth.

Your two eyes enable you to see depth because each eye takes in a slightly different view of the world. A simple experiment will demonstrate this. Hold your finger up, about two inches from your nose, with the nail pointing to one side. Now look at it first with your right eye, and then with your left. Did you see the same thing with each eye? Your answer should be no. What each eye sees is similar but not the same. With one eye you'll see most of your fingernail, with the other you'll see less of it.

It makes good sense that your two eyes won't see the exact same thing, because they aren't located in the same place on your head. Your left eye sees a bit more of what's on the left side of your head, while your right eye sees a bit more of what's on the right. Your brain takes the pictures that it gets from each eye and combines them so that you see not only the front of an object, but a little on each side of it as well.

This special vision, called depth perception, only works with objects that are close to your eyes. When an object is far away, it will look the same to each eye. You can test this for yourself. Find a tree that is about a block away. Now look at it with your right eye first and then with your left. This time you should see the same thing with each eye because you can't see around the sides of the tree when it's that far away. When your brain gets the same picture of an object from each eye, the object won't seem to have any depth. Observing that an object has depth is one way that you know that it is close to us. If an object lacks depth our brains assume that the object is far away.

WHAT HAPPENS WHEN I SLEEP?

If you've ever wondered what happens when your brain tunes out the world and you're snoozing away, you're not alone. Scientists have been curious about this too, and they have studied lots of people sleeping to get some answers.

One important finding researchers have made is that sleep is complicated! By using special equipment to carefully monitor the brain waves and eye and muscle movements of sleeping people, they have learned that sleep has a specific, repeating pattern during a normal night's rest. Moreover, even though you may think the body is quiet during sleep, experts say that at some points, vigorous mental and physical activity is going on.

Here's what really happens when those eyelids get heavy and you turn out the light. Gradually, your body starts to relax and your mind begins to wander. However, you're still vaguely conscious of what's going on. Then, all of a sudden, your brain breaks off contact with the outside world. You don't hear or see anything any more, and under your lids your eyes slowly drift from side to side: You are asleep!

At first, you sleep very lightly and can be easily awakened. If your brain were being monitored for electrical activity, scientists would notice what they call "slow waves with spindle bursts." Very soon, however, you begin to descend into a sounder and sounder sleep. Eventually, the slumber is so deep that it would take someone several minutes to rouse you, if you could be awakened at all. At this point, your brain output has a different look—what scientists call delta waves. Also, your body is completely relaxed and your heart rate and blood pressure have dropped.

After sleeping very soundly for a while, you gradually pass back through the stages of heavier slumber until your sleep is light again. Now, a new phase called Rapid Eye Movement, or REM, sleep begins. It's during this time that dreaming occurs. Scientists call this phase REM sleep simply because the eyes move back and forth rapidly under the lids as though they are looking at something. Actually, it may be that the eyes *are* looking at something— the unfolding events of the dream!

Not only do your eyes dart back and forth during REM sleep, but a lot of other changes take place. Your breathing is irregular and muscles in your face and fingers twitch. Also, the blood flow and temperature in your brain increases, signaling heightened mental activity. If your brain waves were being monitored, they would look very much like those that occur when you're awake. REM sleep is a very busy time!

After a while, the period of REM sleep ends and you begin passing through the stages of lighter to heavier non-REM sleep again. Scientists say that all of us go through this nondreaming, then dreaming, then nondreaming cycle a number of times during the night. However, the amount of time we

BRAIN WAVES

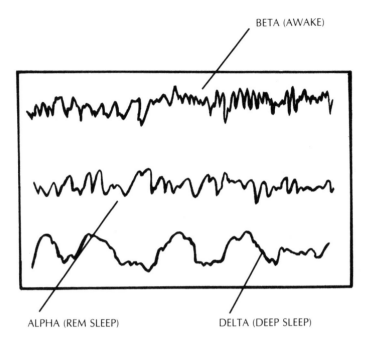

BETA (AWAKE)

ALPHA (REM SLEEP)　　　　DELTA (DEEP SLEEP)

spend in each part of the cycle depends partly on our age. Newborn babies, for example, spend half their snoozing time in REM sleep. (Nobody knows what they dream about!) In contrast, adults usually dream less than two hours a night. Elementary and middle school age children spend more hours than grownups in deep, nondreaming sleep, perhaps because this is the time when the largest amounts of the chemicals that stimulate their growth are released in the body.

Now you have a good idea what goes on during sleep. But if you're wondering *why* all this happens, you'll have to wait! Scientists are still searching for the answers themselves.

WHY DO I GET HEADACHES?

A headache may *feel* like a pain in the brain, but it really isn't that at all. The truth is, the soft tissues that form your brain cannot feel any pain.

A headache actually arises from pain in the muscles of your head and neck. These are the same muscles you use to smile, chew food, wrinkle your nose and turn your head. Head pains can also occur in the blood vessels that lead to these muscles.

Scientists have identified several different kinds of headaches. Muscle tension headaches are most common. They occur when muscles in your head and neck tighten for long periods of time. Muscles tighten and change shape as they work. You can feel this for yourself in your jaw muscles. Place your fingers at the back of your jaw, about one inch in front of your ear. Now bite up and down with your teeth. You should feel your chewing muscles change shape. When working muscles change shape, they can press on blood vessels and cut down on blood flow to the nearby muscles. When this occurs for long periods of time, the blood-starved muscle cells produce a chemical that turns on your pain neurons, creating a headache. In a way, the headache is like a warning flag telling your brain that something is wrong.

All sorts of things can cause muscle tension headaches. When some people get tense, for example, they unconsciously tighten up their jaw or neck muscles and soon develop a head pain. Reading in poor light, or staring at the TV for long periods can also cause headaches, as overworked eye muscles get tired and produce pain chemicals.

THE SINUSES

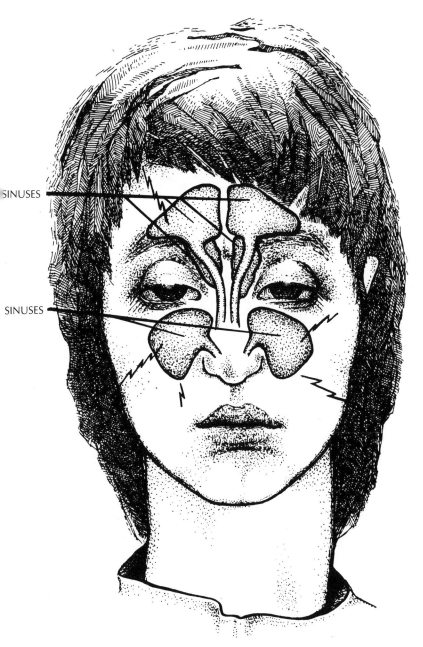

SINUSES

SINUSES

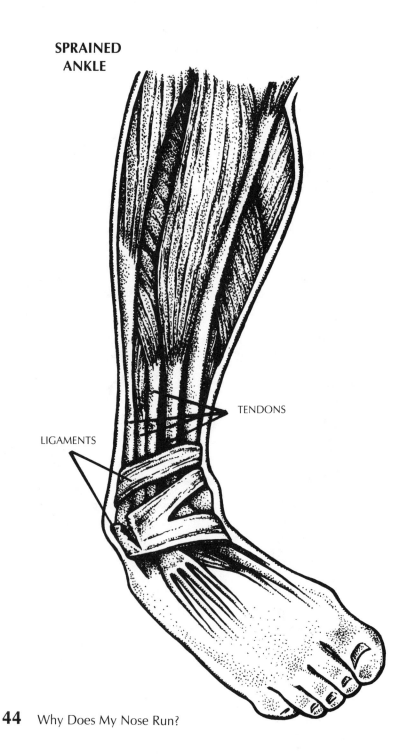

SPRAINED ANKLE

TENDONS

LIGAMENTS

A second type of headache, the vascular headache, results from the stretching of blood vessels. Certain chemicals can cause our blood vessels to expand more than normal. These blood vessels have pain neurons in their walls. As the blood vessels stretch so do the neurons. The stretched neurons send a message "PAIN" to the brain. A surprising number of foods have chemicals that can cause vascular headaches in some people. These include the chemical nitrites found in hot dogs, bacon and salami, monosodium glutamate found in soy sauce and oriental foods, and chocolate.

A third kind of headache occurs in our sinuses. The sinuses are spaces in the bones of our skull that lie under our eyes and near our noses. Like our nasal passages, these spaces fill with mucus when they become irritated or infected. As the mucus builds up, it presses on the walls of the sinuses causing pain.

WHAT HAPPENS WHEN I SPRAIN MY ANKLE?

You can't make your foot turn around and point backwards. You can't even make it point sideways, without turning your whole leg. If you happen to be running and your foot does get twisted to the side, you'll end up with a sprained ankle.

When you get a sprain, it means that you've stretched or torn one of the ligaments that holds your bones together. Ligaments are tough, ropelike bands of tissue that attach bones to bones. Ligaments can be bent and twisted like a stick of gum can, but if you twist them too much they will tear just like the stick of gum.

There are 206 bones supporting the human body and every place where two bones meet there is a joint. Ligaments stretch between the bones of our joints and assist our muscles in holding the joints together. Now you might be wondering what's the use of having all those bones held together by tissues that can get torn or injured. Why not have one huge bone running through your whole body? The reason is that bones don't bend, only joints do. If your body was held up by one large bone you'd never be able to move it at all. You can see this by looking at your arm. Your wrist has joints in it and so does your elbow, and you can move them easily. The region between your wrist and your elbow, your forearm, however, has no joints, but rather two long bones running inside it. No matter how hard you try, you can't bend your forearm. If you do, you'll break the bones inside. So, your joints and the ligaments that hold them together are very important to you even if they do cause occasional problems.

WHAT MAKES A CUT STOP BLEEDING?

Even if you don't carry a box of Band-aids in your pocket, you needn't go without first aid. Your blood is like an instant Band-aid factory. It can patch up a cut in no time at all!

The factory goes into action as soon as you get cut. Small round structures in the blood called platelets stick to the site of the injury. Upon touching the edge of a torn blood vessel, the delicate platelets break open and give off a healing chemical, called platelet factor. This chemical sets off a series of reactions, which causes the blood to form a waterproof patch or clot. The clot, which plugs up the hole in the blood vessel, is made from many fine strands of a threadlike substance called fibrin. Fibrin also seals the cut skin, drying on its surface to form a hard scab. Usually it takes the blood a mere five minutes to form its sturdy patch. Like a Band-aid, it keeps the blood in and bacteria out.

Over a period of days, the clot shrinks and pulls the torn edges of the cut back together again. Finally, the scab falls off, revealing a smooth patch of newly formed skin.

Sometimes, when a wound is very wide or deep, a clot won't be able to stop the bleeding very well or pull the injured skin together enough. In these cases, it's best if a doctor stitches the skin together to enable it to heal properly. Otherwise, the healed skin will look puckery and scarred.

WHAT MAKES A BRUISE TURN BLACK AND BLUE?

When you cut yourself on the outside of your skin you bleed. A bruise is a cut on the inside of your skin and it bleeds too! The stuff that makes a bruise look black and blue is actually bright red blood! It doesn't appear red to our eyes because we're seeing it through a layer of skin.

Our skin is loaded with very tiny blood vessels called capillaries. When we get bruised, some of

BRUISE

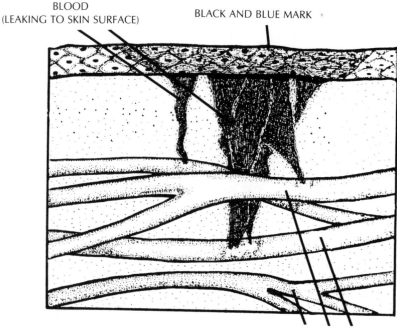

BLOOD
(LEAKING TO SKIN SURFACE)

BLACK AND BLUE MARK

BLOOD VESSELS

these capillaries break and blood leaks out of them into the deeper layers of tissue. If our skin were clear like glass, we would be able to see the spilled red blood as it really is. Our skin, however, acts like a screen. It blocks off some of the light rays passing between the bruise and our eyes. This makes the injury appear to be bluish or purplish instead of red.

Black and blue marks don't keep their colors for very long. After a few days they turn pale. This happens when the leaked red blood cells break down, forming new yellowish substances. Gradually these are reabsorbed by the body and the wound heals, leaving no signs of its colors behind.

WHY DOES MY HEART BEAT FASTER WHEN I'M SCARED OR MAD?

When your heart is pounding in your chest and you're quaking with fear or so mad you think you'll explode, it's a sign your body is becoming fully primed for action.

Strong emotions, such as fear and anger, automatically turn on a special alarm system in your body. Then, almost instantly, various systems gear up so you can run super-fast, fight extra-hard, or take other extraordinary steps that might be needed to handle trouble. Revving up the heart is just one of many ways your body readies itself.

It may seem surprising, but two of the organs that play a major role in preparing your body to meet crises are no bigger than a fingertip! These little dynamos are called the adrenal glands, and each one is located on top of a kidney. Here's how they work.

In response to a strong emotion, your brain excites your nervous system, which in turn stimulates the adrenal glands. The adrenal glands immediately start releasing chemicals, or hormones, called adrenalin and noradrenalin. These have a wide range of powerful, activating effects on the body. For example, not only do they make your heart and blood pressure increase, but they stimulate your liver to start dumping stored-up energy in the form of sugar into your bloodstream. At the same time, the hormones increase your metabolic rate, the pace at which your body burns food. All this helps give the body an extra burst of energy.

Also as a result of adrenalin and noradrenalin, the clotting properties of your blood increase to protect you in case of injury. In addition, digestion slows so energy can be directed to more critical tasks. And the little air storage sacs in your lungs expand, or dilate, so they can hold more oxygen in case you need an extra supply.

Perhaps the most remarkable thing about adrenalin and noradrenalin is that they can accomplish all their work so quickly. In just seconds, they have your body geared up and ready to go. With all the drastic changes occuring inside you, it's no wonder you feel keyed up and notice your heart pounding in your chest!

WHAT HAPPENS WHEN A PERSON FAINTS?

Fainting is your brain's way of saying that it's starving—for blood. Your thinking organ needs a good supply of oxygen-rich blood to work properly. If your brain doesn't get all the oxygenated blood it needs, you're likely to faint.

Normally, your muscular heart does a super job of pumping blood from your head to your toes. How hard it has to work depends on what position your body is in. The job is easiest when you are lying down. The heart must work a little harder when you're standing up because it has to push blood up to your head against gravity.

If you change from a sitting to a standing posture, your heart must adjust its pumping so that it can move blood more forcefully toward your elevated head. This change in the heart may take a few seconds to occur. If you stand up suddenly, the heart may not have enough time to adjust, and the flow of blood to your brain can drop off. This can make you feel a little dizzy and could even make you faint. Usually, however, the heart has adjusted before fainting occurs, and it quickly restores your brain's blood supply to normal.

Things can really get tough for the heart when you stand in one place for a long time. When you walk, your heart gets some pumping assistance from your leg muscles. As these muscles contract to make your legs move, they also help to squeeze some of your blood up toward your head. When you stand still, however, your leg muscles can't assist your heart. After you've stood still for a very long time, some of your blood starts to settle in your feet, and less blood goes to your brain.

Things can get really bad if you're standing in the hot sun. Heat makes you sweat. As your body loses water from sweating, so does your blood. This means that there will be less blood available to go to your head. Thus, if you stand in the sun for a long time you may eventually pass out, falling to the ground in a faint.

Standing in the hot sun isn't the only thing that can cause a person to faint. Hearing some highly emotional news can trigger changes in the body that lead to fainting. Let's say for example that you suddenly learn that you've won first prize in the state-wide science fair. For reasons that scientists aren't quite sure of, all of the excitement causes your brain to react in a special way. The brain stimulates an automatic reaction in your nervous system. A special group of nerves makes your heart slow down and makes the blood vessels all over your body get wider. As more blood goes through widened vessels to your body parts, less blood is available to go to your brain. When less blood goes to your brain, you start to feel dizzy and you can faint.

Although fainting is unpleasant, once you've fallen, things will rapidly get better, because when you're lying down the heart can easily get blood to your brain and you usually recover in a few minutes.

WHAT HAPPENS WHEN I HIT MY FUNNY BONE?

It isn't very funny when you hit your funny bone—in fact it really hurts! And the pain that you feel doesn't even come from a bone, it comes from a nerve in your arm.

The offender is the ulnar nerve, which runs from your shoulder to your pinkie finger, carrying messages to and from your spinal cord and brain. As this long nerve winds its way down your arm, it crosses over a very "bangable" part of the elbow. This hazardous spot is a bony knob with only a thin layer of skin to protect it from bumps. If you examine your bent elbow you can see this point. First, find the tip of your elbow with your fingers. Now move your fingers to the pinkie side of the elbow and up a tiny bit toward the shoulder. You should feel a hard rounded part of a bone. What you are touching is actually the end of the humerous, the large bone that supports your upper arm. The nerve runs over this bump in your humerous.

When the ulnar nerve gets hit it doesn't just hurt in your elbow. The pain you feel follows the path of the nerve down to your last two fingers. Sometimes your ring finger and pinkie will also feel numb for a few moments. Because the ulnar nerve doesn't send any branches to the rest of your hand, however, your other three fingers won't feel anything at all.

THE ULNAR NERVE

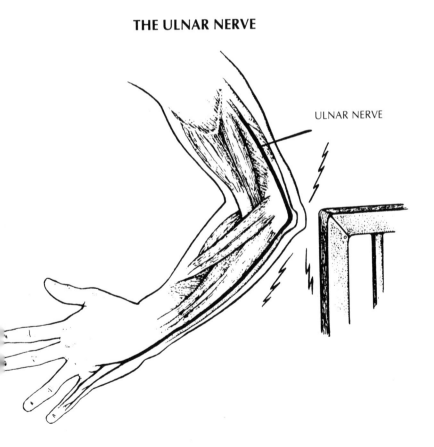

ULNAR NERVE

HOW DOES A BROKEN BONE HEAL?

Your bones are alive and they can heal themselves, just as your skin does. We usually don't think of bones as being alive because they appear solid and unchanging. Actually, though, bones change all the time. Every day old bone cells die and new bone cells form to take their places. Because bone is a living substance, it can easily mend itself.

The healing of bone is something like the healing of skin. When a bone gets broken, new cells start to form very quickly around the break. Our bones even make a kind of temporary bandage called a callus, which, like a scab on skin, holds the bone together during the repair process. A callus, however, does not necessarily keep the bone straight. Our doctors make use of a cast to hold the broken bone in place so that it heals in a nice straight line. A cast may also be designed to put pressure on a bone, because this is known to speed up healing.

Although bone cells grow more rapidly than usual when they are mending a break, repairs still move along fairly slowly. While injured skin can usually heal itself in a few days, injured bones take months to return to normal.

The process of bone healing can be speeded up if the bone can be used during the recovery period. This is because bones, like muscles, grow thicker and stronger when they are used. This is why people often wear leg casts that are designed so that they can walk on the injured leg.

Bones do an excellent job of repairing themselves. Once a bone has healed, it is often impossible to tell that it ever was broken, even with an X ray.

WHAT GOOD ARE FINGERNAILS?

Everybody knows that fingernails are great for scratching an itch, picking up tiny objects and drumming on the table to signal impatience!

But fingernails are also useful in another way you may not have thought about. They protect and provide a rigid backing for the fingertips, which are among the most sensitive parts of our body. Fingertips have thousands of nerve endings that register sensations. If you've ever accidentally banged a fingertip with a hammer or in a door (ouch!), you can imagine just how many nerves the ends of the fingers have. You can probably also imagine how much greater the pain would be if the fingernails weren't there providing a hard, protective shield.

Now you know that fingernails offer protection to a large network of nerve endings, you may wonder why fingertips have so many nerves in the first place. The answer is that they give our fingertips an especially keen sense of touch. Fingertips quickly tell us if something is hot or cold, hard or soft, sharp or dull. Fingertips can also sense shapes and recognize objects. At night, they even help us "see" things our eyes can't make out in the dark—like the covers, the bedpost and the light switch.

To get an idea of how good fingertips are at feeling compared to other parts of your body, try this experiment. Shut your eyes and have someone lay a quarter, a nickel, and a penny on the table. Reach out and touch the coins with an elbow. You can't tell which is which, right? With eyes still closed, touch the coins with your fingertips. Now, it's fairly easy to identify each one, isn't it? That's a lot of sensing power at the ends of your hands!

WHY DO MY TEETH GET LOOSE AND FALL OUT?

Maybe you think that teeth get loose and fall out because the tooth fairy needs a steady job! It's fun to think so, but it's not really the reason.

Losing teeth and getting new ones is something that just naturally happens as you grow. It's one way the body automatically adjusts to your changing size. Gradually, as your mouth outgrows its first set of teeth, they fall out. Then, larger, stronger "permanent" teeth come in and fill the extra space.

Actually, your body has been automatically matching your teeth to your mouth size since before you were even born. In the beginning, when your mouth was tiny, it probably contained no teeth! However, a whole set was ready and waiting in the gums for the mouth to get big enough. Gradually, as it grew, a few teeth came in. Later, a few more, and a few more arrived, until finally, at around the age of two, you had a complete set of twenty "baby" or primary teeth.

When your mouth grew bigger, permanent teeth started coming in to replace them. Eventually, you'll probably have thirty-two in this final

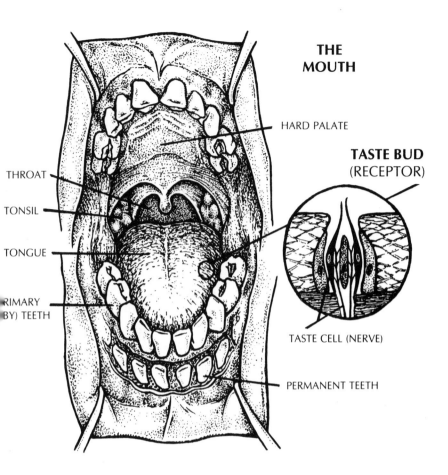

THE MOUTH

HARD PALATE

TASTE BUD (RECEPTOR)

THROAT

TONSIL

TONGUE

RIMARY
BY) TEETH

TASTE CELL (NERVE)

PERMANENT TEETH

set. The last ones, called the wisdom teeth, won't arrive until you're eighteen or twenty and the mouth is full grown. And, if the mouth isn't large enough, they may stay in the gums and never come out at all.

WHY DOES MY STOMACH GROWL?

The digestive tract is a noisy place. It rumbles, it gurgles and it growls. People often think that these strange internal noises are funny, and scientists have given them a name that sounds funny too: borborygmi.

The cause of borborygmi is gas. Gas in the stomach is simply air that gets swallowed along with our food. (Air is actually a combination of gases.) When the stomach contracts, it pushes the gas around, making a great deal of noise in the process. Gas that isn't absorbed or belched out of the stomach may move on to the intestine, gushing and bubbling as it goes.

A loudly growling stomach can be quite embarrassing, particularly in a quiet place like the library. Loud borborygmi result from the strong stomach contractions that occur when we are hungry or nervous. Softer rumblings also occur inside the stomach when it contracts weakly. If you place your ear on a friend's belly, you should be able to hear some of these quieter sounds.

The best way to stop a noisy stomach? It's just what you might expect. A small snack provides the quickest cure for the stomach growls.

WHAT MAKES ME BURP?

A burp is one way your body gets rid of swallowed air. When you sit at the dinner table and gulp down a cheeseburger, you gulp down air too. In fact, any time you eat you swallow air along with the food. If a lot of air gets into your system, your stomach may start to feel very uncomfortable and you will probably burp.

Certain foods and drinks are especially likely to cause burping. These include things like whipped cream and lemon meringue pie, which have air beaten into them, and soft drinks, which are full of gas bubbles. Talking and eating at the same time may also cause you to swallow a lot of air, resulting in a burp.

Not all the air in your stomach leaves through your mouth. Some of it passes harmlessly through your stomach wall and into your blood. The rest moves out from your stomach and on to your intestines. Air in the intestine often leaves your body through your rectum. This is what happens when you pass gas. (See page 60.)

WHY DO I THROW UP?

Throwing up is the very effective way your stomach cleans house! When you vomit, the stomach automatically gets rid of food that for one reason or another it doesn't want to handle. This reflex action can happen when you eat something that is spoiled or very irritating to the stomach lining. It can also occur when you have a virus that disrupts the digestive process.

Actually, it's not the stomach but the muscles at either end of it that work with your brain to bring about this unpleasant emptying action. In response to a command from the vomiting center in the brain, the sphincter, a muscular ring that separates the upper end of the stomach and the food tube, or esophagus, relaxes. Then, a quick, powerful, pushing action by the walls of the abdomen and the

THE DIGESTIVE SYSTEM

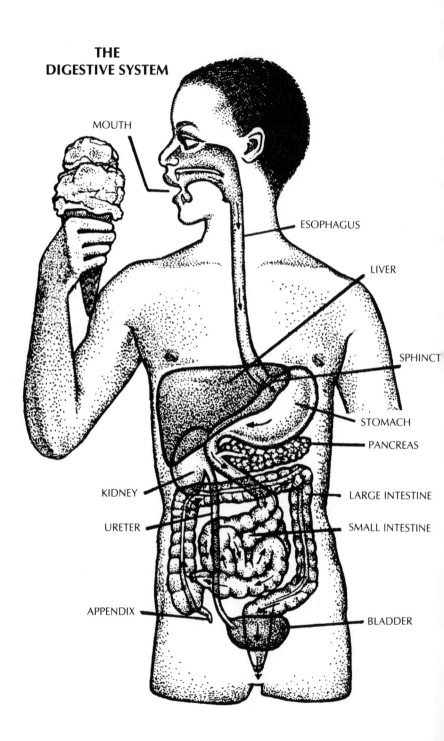

MOUTH

ESOPHAGUS

LIVER

SPHINCT

STOMACH

PANCREAS

KIDNEY

LARGE INTESTINE

URETER

SMALL INTESTINE

APPENDIX

BLADDER

breathing muscle, or diaphram, force the stomach contents up the food tube toward the mouth. You know what happens next!

If vomiting is the body's reaction to irritating material in the stomach, you might wonder why people get car, air or sea sick. The fact is, motion sickness isn't caused by stomach problems at all—it's the result of activity within the brain! Let's see why this is so.

As you probably already know, all body movements are noticed by the special motion-sensing cells within the organs of balance near the inner ear. These cells then send "motion" messages to an area of the brain called the pons. Motion messages alert the brain so it can direct the muscles to make adjustments and maintain balance. (See pages 31 & 33.)

In some people, the constant jiggling or swaying that occurs during car, air or sea travel tends to overstimulate their motion-sensing cells. These cells then send so many activating messages that some of them "spill over" from the pons and activate the vomiting center in a neighboring area of the brain. Stirring up the vomiting center, of course, means trouble for the stomach. It receives orders to become upset even though nothing is really wrong!

COULD I SWALLOW WHILE STANDING ON MY HEAD?

You certainly could! In fact, no matter how you hold your head, you can still chew and swallow and have your food end up in the right place, your stomach!

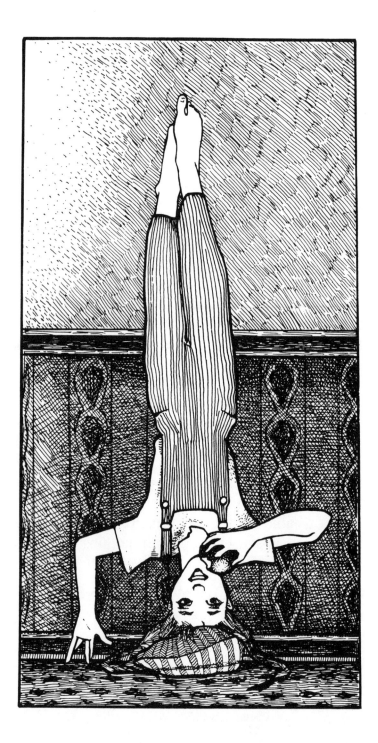

You can swallow upside down because swallowing is a process that does not depend on gravity. You probably know that gravity is the force that holds your body and other objects on the earth and causes things to drop down to the ground rather than up. Astronauts flying in space, where there is no gravity, will float around in their cabins if they are not strapped down. These space travelers, however, have no trouble swallowing even when they're upside down.

Swallowing is a reflex. This means that once you start the process by moving food to the back of your throat, your brain will then take over to complete the job. The swallowing reflex is designed to insure that food goes into your stomach and nowhere else. This is important, because your mouth leads toward three different places; your stomach, your lungs and your nose. Swallowed food could end up in any one of the three, but normally the swallowing reflex prevents this. Here's how.

Each time you swallow, the pathway to your nose and the pathway to your lungs get closed off for a few seconds. At the same time muscles in your throat push food in the only direction left opened, toward the long, tubelike esophagus and on to your stomach. It doesn't matter which way you move your body, the muscles of the throat and esophagus will always squeeze food toward your stomach.

Occasionally food does go the wrong way, particularly when people try to talk or laugh and swallow at the same time. This is what happens when a person chokes. Talking causes the breathing pathway to open, and a bit of food can then get stuck in the windpipe, or trachea. Similarly, if you've ever laughed hard or burped while sipping a soda, you may have experienced the strange sensation of getting the fizz up your nose.

WHY DO PEOPLE HAVE TO GO TO THE BATHROOM?

When a car engine burns fuel, waste material is left over and passes out the exhaust pipe. Human bodies, which use food for fuel, also produce waste and have an "exhaust" system to get rid of it.

Unlike cars, however, people can store up waste before releasing it. Two big advantages of this are convenience and cleanliness. Another reason is that a constant flow of urine or feces from the body would keep the skin damp all the time, eventually causing soreness and infection.

Going to the bathroom is the normal, healthy way we get rid of waste. If we couldn't get rid of it, it would soon poison our bodies. A bowel movement discharges material left when food is processed through the stomach and intestines. The waste, or feces, consists of indigestible plant parts, partly burned foods and other chemicals. The strong odor of feces comes from gasses produced by harmless bacteria that live in our intestines.

Urination gets rid of waste left after the kidneys filter and clean our blood. Urine contains excess water, salts, and a chemical combination called urea.

The feeling of having to go to the bathroom is the body's way of telling us that enough waste is being held. The desire to urinate occurs when our storage tank for urine, the bladder, fills up and starts stretching from the fullness. We know it's time for a bowel movement when the muscles of the intestines start squeezing down on the bulk. This automatic squeezing, called peristaltic contractions, can be triggered by eating or drinking. (See page 60.) That's why we often "have to go" after a meal.

WHY DO I GET THIRSTY WHEN I EAT SALTY FOODS?

It may sound strange, but your body has its own internal supply of special bath water! This watery, salty fluid is constantly needed to bathe the body's billions and billions of cells. Without this bath, they would quickly dry up and die. Making you feel thirsty when you eat a lot of salt is the body's way of insuring that the vital fluid doesn't become too salty for your cells to live in. The feeling of thirstiness causes you to drink more water, which dilutes the level of salt in the fluid.

A part of your brain called the hypothalmus works with your kidneys to keep your cell bath water from becoming overly salty. A special part of the hypothalmus, the osmoregulatory center, constantly checks the amounts of water, salt and other minerals in the cells' "bathing" liquid. Your kidneys control the overall supply of fluid in the body by retaining or passing it out through the bladder.

When the osmoregulatory center of the hypothalmus senses that your internal bath liquid is too salty, chemical messages go out telling the kidneys to hold more water in the body than usual. Messages also go to another part of the hypothalmus called the drinking center. You can probably guess what happens next. You say to yourself, "Boy am I thirsty," and go get a large glass of something wet to drink. When you have drunk enough water to lower the concentration of salt in your body fluid to the right level, the osmoregulatory center stops stimulating the drinking center. Then, you don't have that craving for water anymore.

WHY DO MY FINGERS AND TOES GET WRINKLED WHEN I TAKE A BATH?

Every time you take a bath your skin gets stretched! Yes, the water in your body actually pulls moisture into your skin. The water moves in through your skin most rapidly through the long parts of your body like the fingers and toes. As moisture moves in, the skin stretches and becomes wrinkly.

Skin takes in bath water because of a process called osmosis. Osmosis is the tendency of water to move from a place where it is more pure to a place where it is less pure.

To understand what this difficult concept means let's imagine that we could take a drop of water and enlarge it. If we make the droplet big enough, we will see the tiny building blocks or molecules that it is made of. The first thing that we'd notice is that these water molecules are always moving, bouncing around in the droplet like a room full of rubber balls.

OSMOSIS

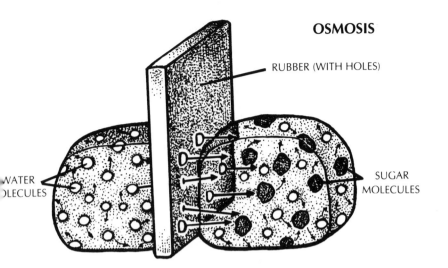

RUBBER (WITH HOLES)

WATER
MOLECULES

SUGAR
MOLECULES

Now imagine that we place a drop of sugar water next to the first drop. The molecules in the second drop, bounce around too, but now there are also sugar molecules bouncing. Next, we put a special piece of rubber in between the two drops, so that it touches both. The rubber is full of tiny holes, just the size of a water molecule, but smaller than a sugar molecule.

What do you think we will see? The bouncing water molecules will pass from one drop to the other through the holes in the rubber while the sugar molecules will remain stuck in the second drop. Since the sugar molecules occasionally get in the way of the bouncing water molecules in the second drop, most of these water molecules will stay where they are. The molecules in the plain drop, however, have nothing to block them, so soon most of them will have moved into the sugar drop.

Now, let's go back to the bathtub. The water in the tub has some particles such as minerals and other substances dissolved in it, but the water in your skin has many more. Thus, the water in the tub is purer than the water in our skin.

Our skin cells are like the rubber membrane because they have tiny spaces between them through which water molecules can pass, but particles dissolved in water cannot. The purer water in the bathtub moves in through the cell layers more rapidly than the less pure water in our skin moves out. This leaves our skin stretched and puckered.

A short time after we leave the tub, our bodies will eliminate the excess water in our urine and sweat, and our fingers and toes will look normal again.

WHY DO I GET CHICKEN POX ONLY ONCE?

If you've ever itched your way through a case of the chicken pox, it's nice to know you probably won't get the disease again. Your body hates being sick as much as you do. So it creates a special army of defenders to fight off the chicken pox virus if it ever comes back. Once that "army," is in place, you'll probably never get chicken pox a second time. The doctor refers to this as having "immunity" to chicken pox.

A virus or any other substance that the body recognizes as foreign is called an antigen. Your body has a whole defense organization, or immune system, to protect it against antigens. First, there are special "lookout" cells, called lymphocytes. These white blood cells circulate around looking out for invaders such as viruses, yeasts and bacteria. Whenever the lookout cells recognize an invader, they send out special chemicals called antibodies to combat the attack. The lookout-type lymphocytes also start growing and multiplying rapidly, so they can produce more and more of these chemicals to join in the fight.

Antibodies locate and attach themselves to invaders. This can harm their enemies in several ways. Sometimes attached antibodies make an invader seem very tasty to special cells in the blood stream called phagocytes. These germ eaters then come gobble it up! Other times, when antibodies attach to a virus, they cover the special spears or sharp points it uses to break into your body's cells.

In effect, this disarms the virus, because it's weapons don't work any more.

Once the battle against a certain kind of invader is over, antibodies against it aren't needed anymore. Many of the lookout-type lymphocytes that produce antibodies die, but some lookout cells live a long time and are good at "remembering" the enemy if it ever returns. A squad of these memory cells remains, keeping you prepared for another attack. As a result, your body can almost always fight off a returning intruder before it makes you sick again. That's why you get chicken pox, German measles and some other diseases only once.

ANTIBODIES VERSUS ANTIGENS

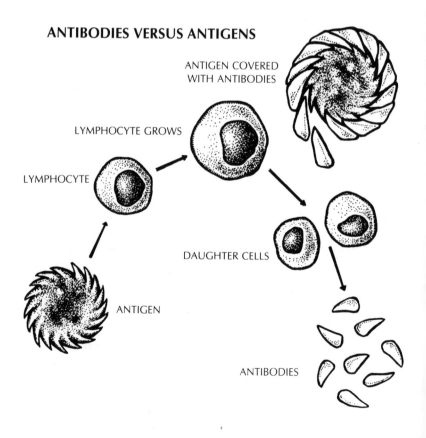

ANTIGEN COVERED WITH ANTIBODIES

LYMPHOCYTE GROWS

LYMPHOCYTE

DAUGHTER CELLS

ANTIGEN

ANTIBODIES

WHY DO I HAVE TO GET SHOTS
WHEN I'M NOT SICK?

You've probably been told that shots called vaccinations protect the body against dangerous illnesses like smallpox and tetanus. But did you know these shots contain specially-treated germs and actually give you a mild case of the disease?

It's hard to believe that being injected with germs could possibly *prevent* illness! But if you've read the preceding part about getting chicken pox, you might be able to guess why this is so.

If you suspect the answer has something to do with the body's immune system, you're right. The body defends best against diseases that have attacked it before. In fact, it's so good at warding off second attacks, you only get many familiar diseases —like chicken pox—once.

The problem is that certain illnesses are so damaging or dangerous that even one attack is too much. So, over the last forty years, researchers called immunologists have developed special chemical solutions, or vaccines, that trick the body into thinking it has a particular disease. This makes it ready in case a "real" attack ever occurs.

The reason vaccines can trick the body's immune system is that they are usually developed right from the disease-causing germs. Sometimes, the germs are killed using a special process. When the "killed vaccine" is injected into the body its germs can't grow and cause illness. But the immune system generally responds as though they were alive. Other vaccines are produced from living germs that are just close cousins of the ones that make you very ill. This type of vaccine is called "live, attenuated." It's sometimes more effective at tricking the immune system, because it actually gives you a mild, nondestructive case of the disease.

WHAT'S AN ALLERGY?

You probably already know that your body has a terrific defense, or immune, system for fighting off enemies like bacteria, yeasts and viruses. But it may come as a shock to learn that in some people this powerful protection system malfunctions and causes trouble!

Specifically, the trouble it causes is an allergy. Oddly enough, an allergy results from the body's defense apparatus trying *too* hard to provide protection! Not only does it wage war on germs and other dangerous aliens that come into contact with a person's body, but it also starts battling harmless, common substances like pollens, animal hair or certain foods. The trouble with this is that during the fighting some of the individual's own cells become inflammed and damaged. Then a runny nose, red, itchy skin, diarrhea or some other equally unpleasant symptom the doctor calls an "allergic reaction" results. This is how it happens.

The basic way the immune system provides protection is to make special germ-fighting chemicals called antibodies. If everything is working correctly, whenever a person's defense apparatus recognizes a dangerous intruder in the body, it immediately starts releasing antibodies into the blood stream to fight off the attack. The antibodies seek out the invader, and it is destroyed. (See page 70.)

When somebody has an allergy, however, the protection process goes haywire. The trouble starts when the individual's defense system mistakenly identifies a harmless substance that happens to come in contact with the body as a dangerous invader. The harmless substance, which doctors call an allergen, might be dust, pollen, a food, feathers, wool clothing, or even a medicine the person is taking! In response to this allergen it *thinks* is dangerous, the immune system sends out antibodies. These circulate around in the blood until they locate the allergen. Often, the antibodies and the allergen meet where the allergen first enters the body—the cells of the skin, or the lining of the nose, lungs or stomach.

At the point when an antibody and allergen come together—BANG!—an explosive reaction takes place, causing ruptures inside the cell. This releases a powerful chemical, histamine, and several other irritating substances that inflame and damage nearby cells. The result is redness, swelling, watery discharge, itchiness and all the other discomforts associated with an allergic reaction. Since histamine is what causes so many unpleasant symptoms, doctors often give allergy sufferers a medication, called antihistamine, that works against it. When allergies are severe, there are also some effective long-term treatments to help lessen the allergy patient's reaction to certain allergens.

What makes the immune system foul up in the first place, you wonder? Nobody is really sure. Researchers do know that the tendency toward allergies is hereditary. So, if you have an allergy, there's a good chance you inherited it from one or both of your parents, and that you might pass it on to your own children someday.

WHAT MAKES A MOSQUITO BITE ITCH?

We don't usually feel much when a mosquito settles on our skin for a sip of blood. Once the mosquito has gone, however, we certainly do notice the results of its visit: a small itchy bump, or mosquito bite.

The itchiness of a bite results from the way that our bodies react to mosquito saliva. Saliva is one of several weapons that a female mosquito uses to get herself a meal. Unlike the male mosquito, who is not a bloodsucker, the female has piercing and saw-ing tools, which she uses to make a hole in her victim's skin. Once she has pierced a blood vessel, the hungry insect injects saliva into the wound. The saliva thins the victim's blood. This enables the mosquito to suck up her meal much the way people suck up a soda through a straw.

Although it helps the mosquito, the saliva can be quite annoying to humans because we are often allergic to it. This means that our bodies react to the mosquito's saliva much the way they would to invading bacteria. Our blood sends the germ-fighting chemicals called antibodies to the site of the bite. In some way that scientists don't yet completely understand this antibody activity affects nerve endings in our skin, making us feel itchy. (See page 70.)

We all get mosquito bites once in a while, but some of us seem to get more of them than others do. It turns out that mosquitos prefer to dine on certain kinds of humans. The favorite victim of a hungry mosquito is a sweaty woman wearing dark clothes and perfume.

WHY DO BROTHERS AND SISTERS OFTEN LOOK ALIKE?

You probably already have a general idea why the children in a family tend to look alike. It's because they have the same parents and have inherited some of the same characteristics.

But just how do parents pass on traits to a child? It may be hard to believe, but the entire bundle of features that make up a person is transmitted in only two tiny cells! One cell, contributed by the mother, is called the ovum. The other, provided by the father, is called the sperm. Each of these special reproductive cells contains half of a complete plan, or genetic blueprint, which will determine the makeup of the offspring. The two halves of the blueprint join together when the ovum and the sperm unite during conception. At this time traits such as eye and hair color and the blood type of the baby are permanently set.

To really understand how the two human reproductive cells furnish the blueprint for a new person, let's take a closer look at them. The nucleus of each contains tiny, threadlike particles called chromosomes. The chromosomes, in turn, are made up of hundreds of even smaller particles called genes. (See page 78.) Scientists say it is the complex chemicals of the genes that actually control the makeup of the offspring. The processes involved in this control are so remarkable and complicated that a whole area of science, called genetics, is devoted to studying how genes work.

It's not only important to know that the reproductive cells contain chromosomes and genes, but to note how many of these particles they have. All normal human cells *except* the ovum and sperm contain forty-six chromosomes arranged in pairs. In contrast, the normal ovum and sperm contain exactly half that number, or twenty-three chromosomes each. If you're suspecting that the chromosomes of the reproductive cells pair up during conception to make the usual total number of forty-six, you're absolutely right! The union combines the genetic material of the two parents and yields a new forty-six-chromosome cell. This cell, called a zygote, grows, divides and, finally, forms a new human being.

HOW DID I GET TO BE A BOY OR A GIRL?

Your father determined your sex! Now this doesn't mean that he actually *chose* whether he wanted a girl or a boy baby. It just means that the characteristics he automatically passed on to you determined whether you turned out to be a girl or a boy. Here's the way it works.

At the time a new human life is about to be formed, there are reproductive cells present from both parents. As you might already know, the mother furnishes an egg cell called an ovum. Reproductive cells furnished by the father are called sperm. In a very complicated way, some tiny thread-like particles called chromosomes within the ovum and sperm determine many things about the child, including its sexual characteristics. Each re-

MEIOSIS

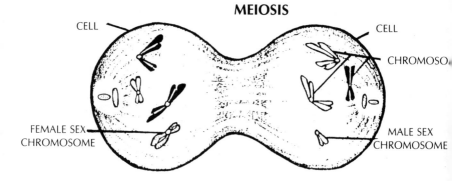

CELL

CELL

CHROMOSO.

FEMALE SEX
CHROMOSOME

MALE SEX
CHROMOSOME

productive cell contains twenty-three chromosomes, half of the forty-six found in all other normal
human cells. When conception occurs, the twenty-
three-chromosome egg combines with a twenty-
three-chromosome sperm to form a new forty-
six-chromosome cell. This cell, or zygote, grows and
divides to form a new person.

To find out exactly what makes a child turn out
to be a girl or a boy, we need to look more closely
at two particular chromosomes. One of these is in
the ovum, and one is in the sperm. Called the sex
chromosomes, these two contain all the characteristics associated with maleness or femaleness of the
new human being. In the ovum, the sex chromosome is shaped like an X. Scientists have learned
that this shape is associated with femaleness. Now
you might be thinking, well of course it is, because
it comes from the female parent. But don't jump to
any conclusions yet! The fact is, about half of all
sperm have the X-shaped chromosome associated
with femaleness, too. The other half of the sperm
cells have a sex chromosome shaped like a Y, which
is associated with maleness.

Now, are you beginning to see how the father could be responsible for his child's sex? If one of his sperm with an X-shaped sex chromosome happens to unite with the ovum, the offspring has two XXs and turns out to be a girl baby. If a sperm with a Y-shaped sex chromosome unites with the ovum, the offspring has an X and a Y and will be a boy. So, even though a new person grows and develops inside its mother, the father always provides the material that makes it a girl or a boy.

INDEX

Illustrations are indicated in **boldface**